Think Like a Photographer!

(and shoot better pictures)

FRANK L. GREENAGEL

with photos by Frank L. Greenagel and Alison M. Jones

for Marley

For information contact:

Mondo Publishing
980 Avenue of the Americas
New York, NY 10018

Visit our website at www.mondopub.com

Printed in China

07 08 09 10   9 8 7 6 5 4 3 2 1

ISBN 1-59336-766-X

Cover and Interior Design by Witz End

Library of Congress Cataloging-in-Publication Data available upon request.

Table of Contents

Introduction

Almost everybody wants to be a photographer. When an old steam locomotive started weekend excursion rides a year ago, the people with cameras outnumbered the passengers. Even at weddings, where there is usually a professional photographer, many guests carry cameras, and flashes mark every act and declaration of the ceremony.

The fact that you have picked up this book means that maybe you'd like to take pictures, too. Perhaps you've never even held a camera before, and you're starting from scratch. Well, this is a great time to begin. I didn't start until I was in high school, and I never took it seriously until I was about 30 years old. Or maybe you've been taking pictures for a while, and friends have told you that some of your shots are pretty good. I hope you want to take your skill to the next level. Whatever your level of experience, you'll find something in here that will immediately and permanently improve your photographs. That's a promise.

The repetitive pattern of the pews is something we naturally respond to. But it is the soft, colored light coming through the stained glass windows that makes this a successful image.

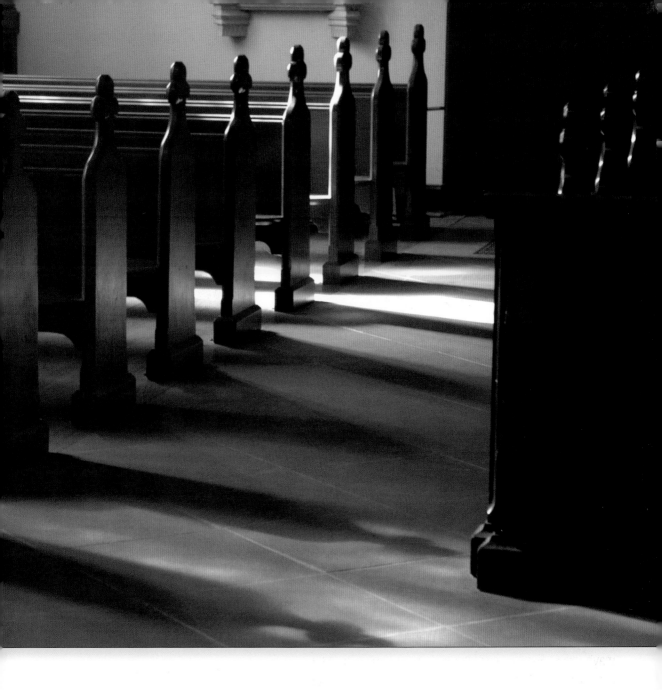

But before we get started, let's pause and think for a moment about all those other photographers out there. How good are most of the pictures they take? The truth is— they're pretty bad. If it weren't for our personal interest in the subjects, we'd even say they were boring. We often overlook that fact, because we are interested in the subject of the photographs—our friends and relatives, a pet, a soccer game, or our trip to the amusement park. But those kinds of pictures are *snapshots*, not good photographic images. As a record of a family picnic or the cute animals you saw at the zoo, they serve a purpose. But if you weren't there, they can be pretty meaningless.

WHAT IS A GOOD PHOTO?

Once you learn to look closely, you'll see that many snapshots are not only boring, they are also poorly composed. The subject is too far away, faces are in shadow, there's no action, the camera was tilted, or the subject is out-of-focus. In most snapshots, there is nothing interesting to grab your attention. And even when there is, simple mistakes often flaw the image.

These two landscapes were shot on the same day within a few miles of each other in North Carolina. One of them is a pretty good image, and the other is uninteresting. The clouds have something to do with it, but the curve of the shoreline, the old building on the point, and the light patch of sand in the bottom image create a unified composition we can understand. The top image lacks any pattern to the trees or the shoreline—there is no strong visual element to draw our attention.

A good image, on the other hand, both attracts and holds your attention, even if the subject is not one you'd have thought was fascinating. We are easily drawn to images of things we're interested in—movie stars, race cars, cats and dogs, friends—but a striking arrangement of light and dark objects, especially vivid colors, or an unusual perspective that makes us look closer can also grab our attention. One of the most memorable photographs of the last 20 years appeared on the cover of *National Geographic.* It was a young girl in Afghanistan whose eyes stare right into you. Look at the close-up on page 45, and you'll get an idea of what I mean.

■ **The curved pattern of the rails seems to emerge from a common starting point and spread out before us—a strong visual element that is impossible to ignore.**

CORRECTING COMMON MISTAKES

Tip Look closely at each of the images before you read the caption and see if you can tell what the major problems are. Then read the caption and decide whether you agree.

There are many ways to improve your picture-taking, but the first step is to eliminate the most common mistakes. Doing that won't instantly turn you into an award-winning photographer, but it *will* put you way ahead of most of your friends and family. To eliminate mistakes, you have to be able to recognize them. So let's take a look at—and criticize—some pictures taken by photographers who either didn't know better, or who didn't think about what they were doing. You may find them all boring, but they also exhibit one or more common mistakes.

The young man with the skateboard was quite self-conscious when I asked to take his picture. In the image on the left, he's sitting pretty stiffly, facing straight ahead. Once I got him to talk about his skateboarding exploits, he loosened up, let his foot play with the skateboard, and even made a few gestures with his hands. The image on the right is certainly more lively than the one on the left.

1 THE CAMERA POSITION IS NOT GOOD.

- The subject is too far away.

- The camera is tilted.

- The subject is not in sharp focus.

- There is a distracting element in the foreground or background that draws attention away from the subject.

In the picture at left, the composition is pretty good. The curve of the body and the dark background behind the head is effective. But the gecko is out of focus, so the image is a failure. Nobody wants to look at a fuzzy gecko. In the image below, the gecko is in sharp focus, and the photographer moved in closer. Check the glossary for the term *depth-of-field*, then look at these images again and consider the importance of depth-of-field in this image.

2 THE LIGHT ON THE SUBJECT IS NOT GOOD.

- The subject is either washed out or too dark.

- The light falling on the subject is uneven or dappled.

- The light is coming from the wrong direction, creating bad shadows.

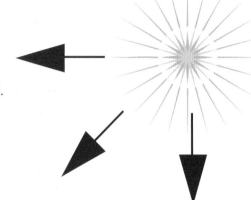

In the image on the left, I wanted to include something of the setting. But the flag was not nearly as bright as the background, so it gets lost. Before taking the image on the right, I moved a few steps and shot towards the house. I had to adjust the exposure a bit, but in this case, the flag stands out brightly against a gray background. Same day, same location, just a movement of a few steps and a slight change in exposure.

3 THE SUBJECTS ARE POORLY POSED.

- There is no action, props, or drama.

- The subject is too far away. (Yes, I know I already mentioned that, but it is worth repeating.) There will be many times when you need to pose your subject, but try to have them doing something other than staring at the camera. Even if he's blowing his nose, that makes for a better image than just having him stand there.

◄ ─ ─ ─ ─ ─ ─ ─ ─ ─ ─ ─ ─ ─ ►

In the top picture, the climber has achieved his goal and made it to the top, but we see only part of his head, and the bright yellow bars are terrible. In the photo on the bottom, his entire body can be seen against the gray background, and we get more of a sense of the effort he has put in. It is essential to take a lot of pictures when you are trying to capture some action, because things happen so fast that it's difficult to know when you've gotten a good shot.

If you can learn to recognize these flaws when you see them in a picture, that's a good *first step* to taking better photographs. When you are aware of these problems, you are more likely to avoid them yourself as you look through the viewfinder of your camera. Most of us are too polite to criticize someone else's pictures, but that's what we're suggesting you do here.

SOME OF THE BASICS

Now let's review some important tips that will eliminate the worst kinds of errors from your images.

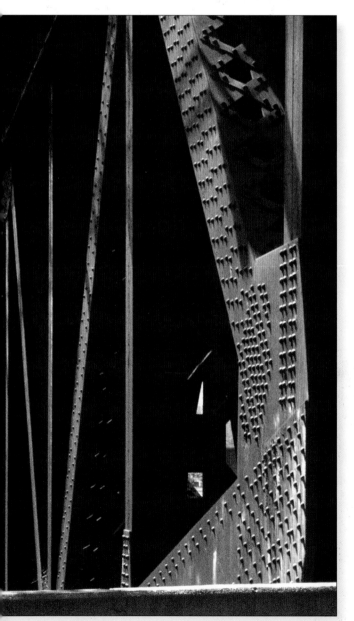

1 SHOOT WITH THE SUN TO YOUR SIDE OR YOUR BACK.

If you shoot looking into the sun, your camera will misread the light, and your exposure is likely to be wrong. That means your subject will be underexposed (too dark). Usually you will find that overhead sunlight is not very good either—early morning or late afternoon light normally results in better images than those shot at midday. The reason is that overhead sunlight usually creates unpleasant shadows and washes out much of the color in the subject. Light coming from the side of a subject is usually better than light coming from directly behind you; it gives kind of a 3D effect to your images because the shadows fall across your subject.

Tip If you have to shoot towards the sun, keep it out of your viewfinder. You might use a tree or building to block it. But sometimes you just have to point the camera down or move in closer.

■ The strong light coming from above and in front of the camera gives a 3D effect to the rivets of the bridge. Soft, indirect light would have left us with a mushy image.

② ISOLATE YOUR SUBJECT AS MUCH AS POSSIBLE.

If all kinds of things are crowded into the image, your real subject may get lost, unless it is a dominant color, strongly lighted (like it has a spotlight on it), or clearly defined in some other way. Sometimes you'll have to wait until other people or cars, for example, move out of the way. But the smarter course is to just shift your position a bit and shoot from a different angle.

■ The Museum of Modern Art in New York City provided this opportunity to capture a visitor waiting for her companion. Unposed shots of people are called candids. The individual, usually unaware of the camera, is just being natural.

■ Two rocking chairs on a freshly painted porch might not seem worth shooting, but the image may have inspired pleasant associations (home, grandma and grandpa, strawberry shortcake) to the photographer and to other viewers. The wicker rocking chairs stand out clearly from the background, but the photographer had to move in close to exclude a white window frame and a bright brass lamp on the wall.

3 MOVE IN TO FILL THE VIEWFINDER WITH YOUR SUBJECT.

The *details* of your subject usually provide the interest. Long eyelashes, a white spot on a puppy's nose, the texture and color of lichen growing on a rock, or the gleam that reflects light back from a well-oiled machine—these types of things make images memorable. You don't have to include *all* of the building, the face, or the flower. Sometimes just enough to *suggest* the subject is enough. A famous photographer (Robert Capa 1913–1954) once said, "If your photos aren't good enough, you're not close enough."

■ The face of this Yankee fan was in shadow, but it was evenly lit, so shadows created no problems. The camera's mode was set for *portrait*, which makes the background a bit out-of-focus. That's deliberate. That way, anything in the background becomes less distracting.

■ The portrait of this young clown is unacceptable because of the dark shadows on her face. It would have been better to photograph her in the shade, probably with fill-flash to keep the colors vivid.

 Light and shadow can work for or against a photographer. Consider these two images. In the image on the right, the shadows break up the architectural elements of the subject. In the image on the left, we see how the strong, sharp shadow of a tree across a building makes the photo much more dramatic. The image was shot in black-and-white because the only bit of color is the foliage in the lower right corner, and that would have been distracting.

Tip Unwanted shadows are the major reason for poor portraits. You many not notice the shadows under a cap's visor or below the eyebrows or nose when focusing, but the resulting dark areas jump right out at you when you see the print.

4 CHECK THE SHADOWS AND THE CONTRAST.

If you're shooting a portrait of a friend, you would normally make sure that the face is evenly lit, not partly in shade and partly in sunlight. If important elements of the subject are in deep shade or shadow and others are brightly lit by the sun, you will probably be disappointed, because the contrast between the light and dark areas will be too great. Either you'll lose all texture in the bright areas (they become solid white) or you'll lose detail in the shadow areas (they become solid black). Sometimes you can use that type of high contrast for dramatic effect, but usually it results in a flawed image.

5 CHECK THE EDGES AND THE BACKGROUND FOR DISTRACTING ELEMENTS.

You don't want a tree growing out of Aunt Margie's head. Even a white van in the background (or at the edge of your image) is distracting. You generally won't notice it when you are looking through the viewfinder because you are intent on the subject. But when you see the print later, you'll say, "Ohmigosh, I never saw that," and you'll toss that print away.

Tip Take your time. After you've taken the picture, check it in the viewer. Then shoot it again to eliminate even minor problems or to change your perspective.

■ **Your eye always goes to the brightest element in the picture. The white car parked in front of the dark church is very distracting—you almost have to look at it first, instead of concentrating on the church. By shifting his position, the photographer was able to exclude it. The dark car in the foreground is not a problem.**

6 GET THE IMAGE AS SHARP AS POSSIBLE.

Your digital camera will probably focus for you, but if you move while you are pressing the shutter release, the image will not be sharp. Your viewers will accept a lot of blurred motion if you are shooting a soccer game, but not if it's supposed to be a picture of an old stone building or a portrait of your little sister.

⑦ MAKE SURE THE HORIZON IS LEVEL.

You do that by keeping the camera as level as you can. It is very distracting to see the horizon tilted as though the buildings are about to slide off to one side. You should also consider rotating the camera 90 degrees to create a vertical image if the subject is taller than it is wide. A church steeple, for example, should rarely be shot with the camera in a horizontal orientation. Turn it on its side, then move in until the church and the steeple fill the frame. There may be situations that benefit from a tilted horizon, but then it should be *really* tilted, not just a little bit, or people will think you don't know what you're doing.

■ The light was directly overhead in the shot on the left, so the building is not well lit. In the above image, the afternoon sun is behind the right shoulder of the photographer, so it lights up the building very nicely.

Sometimes photographers get so excited about a subject that they don't look closely at what is in the viewfinder. Perhaps they fail to notice the shadows falling on the subject, or a distracting object near the edge of the frame. One step to better photography is to take time to think about what you are doing *as you compose the image*. Spend a few extra seconds looking at all four edges as you frame it in the viewfinder. Then look again at the composition—the *arrangement* of forms and shapes, of light and dark areas—not the actual subject of the picture. That may sound a little hard to remember, but I'll help you try in the next two chapters.

If you have never used anything more complicated than a disposable camera before, you might want to turn to the last chapter of the book (page 56) where you'll find a basic orientation to digital cameras. If you already know the difference between a lens and the shutter release, let's get started right now. You can learn about the camera after you've had a little experience with it.

CHAPTER 1

Composition

Walking around hoping something will catch your eye rarely works. Yet it is important to explore and experiment with your camera. So where do you begin? Two things have worked for me. One is to start with things that interest you—it might be birds, or lighthouses, or signs—really almost anything. In my case it has been religious architecture, but even everyday things like T-shirts hanging on a rack can result in a terrific image. So if you have an interest in a particular subject, go for it.

The other way is to look for strong visual elements—bold lines, serious shadows, shapes, and textures. Those visual elements don't usually jump out at the untrained eye, but once you are alert to them and you start looking for them, you will begin to see interesting visual elements all over the place.

In the Introduction, we talked about how essential it is to avoid the common mistakes that mar so many pictures. But to make really memorable images, you have to go beyond simply avoiding mistakes. You need to be aware of the elements of composition and learn to "see" in a new way. That's our task in this chapter.

■ **By excluding everything but a small portion of two columns, I force the viewer to concentrate on the lines and shapes I've selected. There is very little color in the image, but the curve of the base of the one column provides some contrast with the verticals in the rest of the image. The lighting is soft, as the picture was shot on a hazy, overcast afternoon.**

A couple of vivid colors jump out from the more subdued hues. The image is a very simple one—a series of irregular, vertical "strips" of color is the main element. If the strips were all the same width or shape, the image would be boring.

This is just a portion of a spinning wheel, but the spokes and an arc of the wheel are lit from the side. Those bright lines against a rather plain background are much more interesting than if the wheel had been lit from the front. This is an example of how a partial view, even though it doesn't give us much information about the spinning wheel, results in a better composition, just because of its simplicity.

ELEMENTS OF COMPOSITION

Photography was invented in about 1839, and many astonishingly good images were made, even with crude equipment, over the next few years. Part of the reason is that over the centuries, artists had worked out some basic principles—visual elements to consider when composing a painting. Photographers soon adapted those principles when making their own images. We usually refer to them as *elements of composition*.

Composition is basically the selection or arrangement of objects—what you include or exclude when looking through your viewfinder. Composition also refers to the light and dark areas in the image, to strong colors, and to the lines and shapes you've included, if they are strong enough. A photograph of an old steam locomotive from the side is just a snapshot of a locomotive. But it might be a pretty good image if you were careful to eliminate the common errors and the light is coming from the side. If you move in very close to the drive wheels, you'll see the image now is dominated by an arrangement of circles and lines and rectangles, perhaps with different textures as well, all emphasizing the form of the steel wheels and pistons and shafts. At that point we can say with some certainty that you were consciously aware of composition. And that image is likely to be honored above all the others.

Few images will include all of the following elements of composition. But if you actively look for them as you compose your shots, you are likely to produce many more photographs that are not merely snapshots, but which have several visually interesting elements.

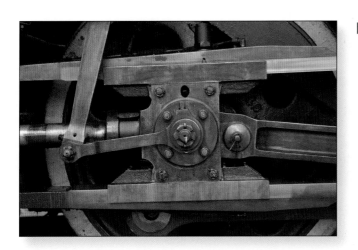

■ Note the strong lines and shapes of the drive wheel of a steam locomotive in this very tight view. At first, it looks like a black-and-white print. But if you look closely, you will find a lot of color in parts of the image. The columns on page 19, the spinning wheel, and this image would work well as black-and-white images (*monochrome* is the word we might use), but many of the pictures elsewhere in this book depend on color for at least some of their effectiveness.

1 LIGHT IS THE MOST IMPORTANT ELEMENT TO CONSIDER.

Photographers describe light as being *hard or soft*. Hard light comes from a single point (the sun or a flash or an unshaded light bulb) and may create dramatic shadows that fall across the subject. Hard *side* lighting is usually exciting, but if hard light comes from overhead, it may wash out any texture or details. Soft light is *diffused*, such as you would get on a cloudy day, or in fog. Soft light has no particular direction—it seems to come from all directions. It doesn't create a shadow so it's usually best for a portrait when you don't want shadows falling across portions of a person's face. Soft light may also create a sense of *mood*, as a foggy landscape does, because it softens the edges of objects and obscures details of stuff in the background.

A subject that looks dull and undramatic might be a lot more dramatic if strong light comes from the side, creating long and dark shadows. Light that is directly overhead is rarely good for a photographer—so if you don't get up before dawn, you might as well sleep in until late afternoon, when the light gets good again.

There's another aspect of light to be considered—its color. Late afternoon light, when the sun is low on the horizon, is much *warmer* than it is at midday. It will give a rose-colored or even a pinkish tint to most things. When the sun goes down, the color shifts, and shadows become bluer for a while. So spend a moment thinking about where the light is coming from and whether it is hard or soft.

■ Only soft light has filtered in to illuminate the entry porch of this Greek Revival building. Strong direct light penetrating the area would have turned this subdued, quiet image into a high-contrast scene with a very different feeling.

■ The light is strong but not directly overhead, so it lights up enough of this fellow's face to etch it cleanly against the dark background. If the light were coming from behind the photographer, the face would have been evenly lit, and some of the drama of the composition would have been lost.

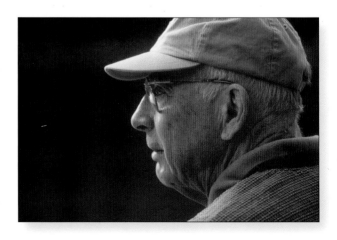

② COLOR CAN BE THE STRONGEST ELEMENT IN AN IMAGE.

There's an old claim that says, "If you can't make the image good, make it red." I don't accept that, but it gives you something to think about. Red is a very dominant color. Often an interesting image is little more than a splash of color rather than the subject itself. In an experiment I tried several years ago, I wandered around a town in France and photographed anything blue. When I found something blue, I had to find something worthwhile about it. That forced me to make a number of colored objects my subjects, regardless of what they were. Many of the images I made that day were awful, but a few were exceptional. Most importantly, it forced me to look and think in a different way than I was used to looking and thinking. Instead of looking for interesting old architecture (or pretty girls), I had to compose my pictures based on the presence of blue. So think color sometimes, rather than objects.

■ The photographer was shooting into a winter sunset, but was careful to keep the sun itself out of the frame. Those are clouds reflected in the water, and it is hard to tell where the reeds end and their shadows begin. Measuring the light to get the proper exposure in these circumstances is tricky. You may have to try several shots before you get it right (see *bracketing* in the glossary).

■ Orange is one of the more intrusive colors, which is probably why hunters are required to wear something orange when they are in the field. Color was the entire reason for the picture, of course, but the rectangular shapes of the framework and the windows in the building reinforce each other. Would the bright color alone have been enough to make this a good image if the background had been a clear blue sky? Maybe . . . but maybe not.

■ The pattern of the curving lines and the apparently irregular placement of the steeple-like ends of the pews—most well-lit but a few very dark—really worked for me.

3 PATTERN AND TEXTURE ARE FAVORITE ELEMENTS OF PHOTOGRAPHERS.

A line of fence posts, the weathered siding of an old barn, a row of trumpets in a marching band, even glasses lined up in the cupboard—these are all good subjects to look for. Repetition intrigues us. Often it is not just a strong pattern, but a break in the pattern that we find interesting, such as rows of closed windows in a old apartment building, with one or two off-center, wide open, with curtains fluttering in the breeze. Sometimes we refer to things like the texture of peeling paint or a coarse fabric as pattern, too. So we can use that term for both the repeated elements in a scene or for an interesting texture, like a brick wall or a rough stone surface.

4 LINE HAS ALWAYS BEEN AN ESSENTIAL ELEMENT FOR
MOST PAINTERS, AND IT IS NO LESS IMPORTANT FOR
PHOTOGRAPHERS.

Obviously there are lines everywhere you look, but most of them are not useful
for the photographer. Try to find lines that are dominant in some way. Light reflecting
off railroad tracks in the late afternoon creates very strong lines that command our
attention. Others have shot these images before, but you should try it, too. They won't
be entirely fresh, but it's good experience to look for strong lines.

Some edges are basically lines, too. They're just wider than the average line, and
they probably outline a shape. What's important is that you look for a line or an edge
or a shape that is both clearly defined and distinct from whatever is next to it. Lines
usually need to be strong to work as a visual element in your composition.

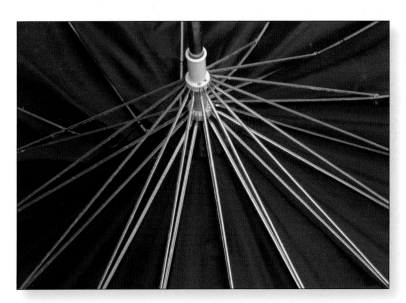

■ A broken umbrella lying on the sidewalk is a photo opportunity if you
are looking for strong visual elements. The bright, radiating spokes
and angles are striking. Imagine if the fabric of the umbrella had a
colored pattern or some advertiser's name on it—a much less effective
image, don't you think? Where do you think the white hub of the spokes
should be placed—a little more off-center, perhaps?

■ Did you ever think that a line
of foam that will disappear in a
moment might be the focus of
a strong image? The surf in the
background against the jagged
rock is nice, but the impact of the
image depends largely on the
uncertain line that runs through
the lower half of the picture.

5 SHAPES, TOO, ARE EVERYWHERE. BUT INTERESTING SHAPES ARE DEFINED IN A COUPLE OF WAYS.

One is the way in which light emphasizes the shape, such as when it "falls off" the edge of a round object like a pear or an egg or a silo (okay, the last one is *cylindrical*, but you know what I mean), Another is when areas are considerably lighter or darker than their surroundings, such as the window in the image below at left, or a darkened window or doorway where the rectangle is in sharp contrast to the rest of the room. Any shape *silhouetted* against a lighter background is usually the significant element in a picture.

Whenever you have an important element, such as a dominant color or a strong shape, you must consider *where* you place that object—a little to the left or right of center rather than dead-center is often effective. But try it more than one way and make your own decision. Don't just settle for the first shot you take. Shoot it again, placing it in different sections of your viewfinder. Then shoot it again! Take at least six different shots of a subject.

■ Shapes don't have to be regular polygons, of course. They can be human figures, skylines, or a tree. The backlit scarlet leaves of the maple at right provide an unusual way of silhouetting the twisted trunk.

■ The dominant element in the image at left is the shape of the window, strengthened by the outside light. A second element—a very subtle one— is the small patch of light on the floor, which our brain connects with the window. Notice that the window is not rectangular. It is called a rhombus (four sides, with one pair of opposite sides parallel; a rectangle has both pairs of sides parallel). I think the rhombus is a more interesting shape than if the window were a rectangle. The window is not in the center of the image, but is off to the left. Why do you think the photographer did that?

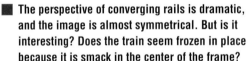 The perspective of converging rails is dramatic, and the image is almost symmetrical. But is it interesting? Does the train seem frozen in place because it is smack in the center of the frame?

■ This is a bolder image, with strong yellow lines on black. Which do you like better? A very important bit of advice: make sure the train is not moving before attempting this.

6 PERSPECTIVE IS AN EXCEPTIONALLY USEFUL ELEMENT FOR A PHOTOGRAPHER.

You know how buildings and other figures seem to get smaller as they get further away from you—that's what we mean by *perspective*. Until about the fifteenth century, artists in Europe didn't understand how to represent a three-dimensional object, such as a building or the interior of a stable, on a flat surface. That's why most of their paintings look kind of distorted to us. Then several artists (notably an Italian architect named Brunelleschi in about 1420) worked out rules for drawing perspective. For a generation or two, artists from Italy to the Netherlands made perspective the actual subject or their paintings. Several of them became known for their mastery of perspective. It is not uncommon today to find strong images that depend entirely on perspective for their impact, such as a line of telephone poles along a roadside that diminishes as they recede into the distance.

■ The perspective of the converging rails and the diminishing size of the bridge structure are the dominant elements in this image. Any spot of color might have distracted from the pure geometry of the image, so it was shot in black-and-white.

7 REFLECTION CAN BE FOUND ON A VARIETY OF SHINY SURFACES.

Reflection is rarely mentioned in the classical works on composition, but photographers have made frequent use of images reflected in windows, in water, in someone's eyeglasses, or any shiny surface. Sometimes the reflections distort the images, sometimes they are a mirror copy. Neither is better than the other, so look for reflections and experiment.

■ The bottom half of the picture is almost a mirror image of the top, but the photographer has been careful to include a few stems of grass in the foreground. The break in the skyline indicates a cross street; it is as important as the low-hanging clouds. If this had been a sunny day with a clear blue sky, I doubt that I would have taken the picture.

■ This image consists entirely of reflections in the water. Note the way the ripples break up the geometry of these buildings in southern France. What if the water had been still, and the photographer had included the buildings themselves— do you think that would have been a better or a worse image?

USING THE ELEMENTS OF COMPOSITION

The important thing to remember about these elements is that they can help your images immensely. Even before you look through the viewfinder at your subject, try to find something like a strong line, an unusual texture, a dominant patch of color, or dramatically converging lines, and make that the central idea of the image. As you consider subjects that interest you, look for one or more of these elements. When you see a strong line, perhaps the edge of a bowl or the fender of a car emphasized by a hard side light, you can make that line, rather than the bowl or the car, your subject. A yellow skirt flapping on a clothesline in the midst of white shirts and towels might make a strong image, even if you'd never thought of someone's wash as being even slightly interesting.

■ My eye moved back and forth from the toppled gravestone to the church and back again. Then I noticed the bright white sign to the left of the church, and immediately recognized that the shape of the windows (called a Gothic arch) is the same as the sign and the gravestone. If I had moved in tighter on the church to exclude the gravestone, I would have missed the strong composition of this image.

Tip Sometimes we're attracted to an image because of the information there, but often what grabs us is the composition—that is, the arrangement of light or dark objects, a splash of color, a strong line or shape.

Any discussion of composition would be incomplete without a note on the arrangement of these visual elements. We've said that a dominant element should probably not be placed dead-center in your picture, but the matter calls for more than that bit of advice. Often you need to think in terms of *foreground, middleground, and background.* Landscapes, it seems to me, often benefit when there is something interesting in the foreground. Portraits are usually better when the foreground is sharp, and everything in the background is indistinct and out-of-focus. The challenging thing about photography is that the photographer must often struggle a bit to identify and select interesting visual elements, and then decide where to place them. There is no science to that, and no formula. You have to develop your eye, and that takes practice.

The more you actively see these elements in the world around you, the sooner that vision will show up in your photos. When you consistently make use of those visual elements as you select and compose your subjects, your work will rightly be seen as *photographic images* instead of snapshots. And that's a goal really worth striving for.

■ A picturesque wagon wheel in the foreground is a staple for photographers of the Old West. But here the wheel is broken, and there are only remnants of the buckboard. It seems to me that the wreck is especially appropriate because the shot was taken in the ghost town of Bodie, California. Cover the foreground with your hand and notice how much the image is changed.

What to Photograph

In this chapter I'll provide suggestions about looking for subjects in common situations. Anybody can take an interesting picture at the Great Wall of China or in Yosemite, but what do you shoot in your own neighborhood? There are things to search for when you are out with your camera. Let's begin by considering some photo opportunities you can practice on.

 FRIENDS, RELATIVES, AND PETS

Usually the faces of your friends and family are the important features of your pictures. I say usually, because sometimes it is what they are holding or doing that is more important. Sometimes a person's hands, or his posture, is more expressive than his face.

It is almost always a good idea to get down on the same level as your subject. If you have a long, low dog like a dachshund, get down on the ground to photograph it, rather than shooting from your own height. Where do you think the photographer was when she took the picture of the pigs on page 35? Whether it's a pet or a person, concentrate on the eyes—that's often the part of an image we notice first. It's hard to get a pet to pose for your camera. But if you can have someone play with it, you can move in close and get an action shot. If you are shooting a brother or sister or friends, get them doing something like pointing out the scar on their knee or the gash in their skateboard, or showing how they caught the Frisbee in their teeth (oops, maybe that was your dog). That's going to be more interesting than having someone just looking right at the camera.

Candid pictures of relatives, neighbors, and friends—working or relaxing—are always great subjects. Although both these men are facing the photographer, the shot does not appear posed. It's as though they turned towards the camera in mid-conversation, and the fellow in the foreground is not especially happy about the interruption.

In the late afternoon, several musicians gather in the gazebo in a local park. The background was horrible for a photographer—quite bright, with lots of shapes to interfere with the subject's profile. I moved in tight, opened up the aperture, and used fill-flash to get enough light on the subject. This colorful fellow is a pretty good guitar player. He doesn't play Bach, but he knows every song Hank Williams ever wrote.

The photographer moved in very tight on the subject, controlled the depth-of-field, and caught an expressive moment and a connection between a boy and his dog.

The young boy, caught in an unusually quiet moment, seems unaware of the camera, or at least unconcerned. There is nothing distracting in the background. Everything seems very natural.

I had been taking pictures of my granddaughter for several minutes when I got this picture, so she was used to the camera. And besides, we'd just come from the zoo, and she had several great props. I took many shots, but this was my favorite.

Even when the subject is a pig, it is helpful to get down on eye level. The light is coming from above, but there are enough light and dark areas so that the shape of the pig, and especially its ears, stand out strongly.

Probably the most important things about taking pictures of people are (1) to get close—really, really close, and (2) to take lots of shots. You want to get as close as you can without distorting their nose (which will happen if you really get in their face). And don't stop shooting just because you think you have a good image. Keep the subject talking in order to make him or her less self-conscious, and keep shooting the whole time.

2 SCHOOL ACTIVITIES, SPORTS, AND HANGING OUT

Once you become known for your photographic skills, you'll probably be asked to take pictures of many school activities for the school paper or website. There are a couple of specific things that can add interest to these kinds of images, but try to keep those elements of composition foremost in your mind. If you do, you will almost always come up with stronger images than someone who ignores color, line, shape, and the source of the light.

■ What more could you want than a red, white, and blue color scheme for a parade? The shot was carefully composed, and the background was made less intrusive by throwing it out-of-focus. Shots like this demonstrate the importance of knowing how to control the camera.

One suggestion is to try to include some prop in the scene with the people—a papercutter, a globe, or even a book. (That's right, a book!) People in costumes or colorful uniforms are a natural. If the subjects are doing something, what are they doing it with? Can you tell where the action is happening? Try to include some identifying item, like a poster on the wall or an assignment written on the board. If several people need to be in the shot, get them to interact with each other rather than just look at the camera. One could be pointing out something to the others, perhaps showing how far the ball sailed over the catcher's mitt. In other words, get someone's hands involved.

Often there is a story to tell that requires a series of pictures rather than a single image. If there is a bake sale to raise money for an activity, you can show some of the preparations (mixing the ingredients), then the table where the cookies and brownies are for sale, then someone sampling them or passing money to the vendor. What is the purpose of the fund raiser? Can you get some image of that? A series is often more revealing than a single image when it comes to a school activity, and I don't mean just more pictures of the same people (or different ones) looking at the camera. Look for images of activities taken at different stages of the event with students, parents, or teachers doing something.

3 YOUR WORLD, INCLUDING ARCHITECTURE, TRAVEL, AND LANDSCAPES

Even if you are not traveling to exotic foreign countries, there is certainly much in your neighborhood to photograph. You could start with your room, and work your way through the house, then to the yard or street in front. Then go down the street to the corner, looking at the architecture of the buildings (especially the details), objects in front yards, and maybe the reflection of one car in the hood of the one behind it. Signs are often interesting, and sometimes shop windows, although the reflections can be tricky. Look for color, line, shape, reflection, perspective, and so on. Those are your subjects just as much as the neighborhood is.

Tip Many people try to get everything into the viewfinder. They want to include the entire scene. At least half the time, you should look for details. Move in close and focus on someone's hands, shoes, or even a belt buckle. If you're photographing a building, try isolating a doorknob or even a window molding.

In your neighborhood hamburger joint, pizza parlor, or mall, you may find good color, strong lines or shapes, and other elements that strike your eye. It may seem common to you, but see what you can find. Here we have an inside-outside scene. Bright patches of light on the empty seats and the countertop provide a sense of depth to the interior.

There's no rule that says you have to include the entire sousaphone. Notice the several strong geometric elements: the curve of the horn, the horizontal lines of the tubing, and the angled row of the three pearl keys.

■ Thousands of snapshots of Yosemite's Half Dome are made every day. This view dares to be different. A sun-kissed glimpse through the clouds is sufficient, the photographer is saying, to get a sense of the monumentality of this rock.

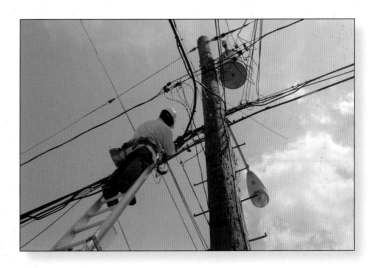

■ There are no perpendicular or horizontal elements in this image, which is a good thing. If the pole and lines and ladder were not running at angles to the sides of the picture, it would be a lot less dramatic.

■ This was shot in an ancient pueblo in New Mexico, where the usual subject would have been the adobe architecture or some of the traditional pottery made by the Indians. But here, the focus is on a plastic toy. It stands out in spite of its very small size because of the bright blue and yellow of the plastic, contrasting with the earth colors of the adobe walls. The diagonal shadow cutting across the top of the image also makes a strong statement.

Tip Think about that colored toy—if you saw it in the clutter of a child's playpen, would you even bother to look twice? Probably not. It's not always the subject of a photograph that attracts our attention. Often we are simply attracted by the combination of color, light, and shape that make up the composition.

On your walk back, shoot only things that are blue (or yellow or red). Make the same walk a few hours later, when the sun is lower in the sky and the lighting and shadows have changed.

If you are shooting pictures for a school publication or for an assignment, people will have certain expectations, and you ought to try to meet them. If they expect an image of the team's trophy for finishing third in their division, get the best possible image of that trophy.

But you may conclude that the subject matter—that is, the trophy, or the building, or the game—is just an excuse for pointing your camera in a certain direction. What you really want to do is to make a memorable image, and in that case, the subject of your photo doesn't matter very much. Take a look at the image of the barrels. It was shot in an old gristmill. The barrels were probably used for storing grain that was to be shipped by canal boat to Philadelphia. But the photographer (me) wasn't really interested in barrels, or grist mills, or how colonial farmers got their grain to market. I was interested in making a fine image, and the light on the barrel rims caught my eye. I wasn't looking for barrels. I was trying to find strong visual elements in an unevenly lit eighteenth century gristmill. Obviously you are going to shoot things that interest you, *but always try to think about what the image will look like*, not about the *object* of your interest. That was probably the toughest thing I had to learn about photography. I still have to remind myself.

The elliptical shape of the barrels in the side light was irresistible. Notice that the photographer was careful to keep the source of the light—the window—out of the image. That area would have been too bright, and so would have upset the "balance" of the composition.

CHAPTER 3

Exploring and Experimenting

You should not feel that you have to make a great photograph every time you leave the house with your camera, regardless of your level of experience. The most famous American photographer (Ansel Adams, 1902–1984) once told me that he made only a couple of really fine images in a year, and he shot hundreds and hundreds of photos every year. This is a time to explore and experiment. Maybe some really good images will happen, but maybe most of them will be horrible. It doesn't matter. This is the way you learn. Each time you pick up your camera, you have a new starting point—one based on what you learned the day before.

Two of the great things about a digital camera are (1) you can see what your images look like right away, and (2) you can delete the ones you don't like. You don't have to go to the trouble and expense of developing the film and printing the images before you get a look at them. So if you made a mistake, or you just don't like them, blow them away! Save only the ones you think might be pretty good.

Having said that, many young photographers have trouble getting started because they don't know what to photograph. We've already offered several suggestions in previous chapters (anything blue, your pet iguana, scenes with perspective, signs and numbers, and so on) but here I'll be a little more systematic about it.

We are given no more than a peek at the copper pot, but it dominates the image, probably because of its color and the strong arc of its handle in a basically linear composition.

① YOU ARE THE FAMILY'S JOURNALIST

As you get really good with your camera, others will increasingly look to you to take pictures of events the family wants to record and remember. The barbecue with the neighbors, the reunion, the trip to the beach, Father's Day, the parade on the Fourth of July, and so on. What do you photograph? The principal characters, of course, but also all the cars lined up in the driveway, closeups of the food, of any gifts, of people talking (or dozing, if the party goes late). Close-ups of musical instruments are usually interesting (especially the reflections in the bell of a trumpet, for example), as are images of food cooking on a grill.

If it's a sporting event, like a soccer match or baseball game, get the setting—the sign that announces the name of the place, a scoreboard, the pile of bats and other equipment, the referee, refreshment stand, the little kids who are playing along the sidelines and not watching the game, and the adults who are talking among themselves and not watching the game either. Try to tell the story of the whole afternoon, not just the action shots of the game. If you're shooting the players, don't worry if you didn't get the horizon level or the players in sharp focus—that blur and tilted horizon may suggest the speed and excitement of the game. Remember to move in as close as you can without getting hit by a ball or ejected from the field for interference. Most of all, get pictures of people. Move in tight, get in their faces; you don't have to ask them to pose (assuming they are family or friends), just move in and take the shot. If you don't know the people, it's best to ask permission first.

This young child is totally intent on what she is doing. In this image, the arms and hands are at least as important as the face. Look behind the child at the wall—the light and dark vertical surfaces divide the image in half, and one half into quarters. The child is in one half and the blocks in the other. Somehow that seems more interesting than if the wall had been a solid tone.

■ If you ever thought that eyes were not important, take a long look at this photo. The dreamy look captured by the camera is . . . a stroke of luck? the result of a strong bond with the photographer? a perpetual state for this child? Who cares? It is an arresting image that required the photographer to move in as close as possible.

■ The photographer's assignment was to find a contemporary version of Tom Sawyer's friend, Becky Thatcher. Here are two views—both formal poses, but the subject appears to be enjoying herself. Which do you prefer?

This image does double-duty as a record of the neighborhood—it shows the presence of a tailor and also the row of houses reflected in the window. Don't worry about the horizontal lines in this kind of picture, but take extra care to get the vertical lines and edges vertical.

The bright yellow apparatus in the background is distracting, but it signals that this is a playground. We have a nice shot of the young girl's face—she is clearly delighted to be photographed. Since the shot was not posed and she was very active, it took at least a half-dozen shots to get this one right.

A good portrait does not always have to show the subject's face. Here, the figure is locked in an embrace with the telescopic viewer. It's enough to characterize her for her family, and presents a delightful image for those who don't know her. Notice how few shapes and colors make up this image. Anything else in the frame—a passing boat, a seagull, another person—would have ruined the composition.

② YOU ARE THE DOCUMENTARY PHOTOGRAPHER OF YOUR OWN LIFE

All your friends, of course, as well as your pets, your room, your brothers and sisters, and even your parents will probably be among your first subjects. But don't forget the street where you live, including the houses of your next-door neighbors, the cars that are usually parked on the street, and where you go for pizza or ice cream. Obviously you want to have photos of your school and maybe your teacher.

Do you have tasks or chores that you are expected to do regularly? Get a shot of the lawnmower. Can you find lines, shapes or colors that might make it much more than a lawnmower? Some of this may seem trivial right now, but in a few years you and your family will treasure these photos.

■ I saw this scene while waiting for my plane in Dallas. The arrangement of forms and colors was so compelling that I bought a disposable camera just so I could take this picture. I knew it would not be great—shot with a plastic lens through a sunscreen that did funny things to parts of the image—but when you think like a photographer, there are some shots you just have to take.

3 YOU ARE THE ARTIST

One of the most important American photographers (Edward Weston 1886–1958) spent months of his life photographing peppers and a few other vegetables, all in black-and-white. He liked the shape of them and the way that light revealed those shapes. A pretty silly way to spend your time, you might say. But Weston was enormously influential, and each one of those photographs today sells for more than $100,000!

In the nineteenth century, a French painter spent weeks painting the same haystack. He painted it in the early morning, and then in mid-morning, and again at noon. Then he painted it in the early afternoon, and in the late afternoon. The sun was moving from east to west, so it was lighting up different parts of the haystack. And the color of the light changes during the day (did you know that before you read this book?), so although the haystack was the same, it looks different in every painting. (The painter's name was Claude Monet, in case you were curious, and the paintings sell for millions.) If you don't have a haystack handy, you could do the same thing with a small bush, or even a tree or your house. Don't change your position or your camera angle. That doesn't mean you have to stand in the same place all day, silly! Just mark where you stood and come back, say, every hour from dawn to dusk and make the same shot. Then, if you print them out and arrange them in order, I think you will be amazed at what you have accomplished. You might also photograph the same tree or building in different seasons of the year.

Tip Many people only take pictures on a vacation trip or at a family celebration. But the everyday things around us are usually just as interesting—if you can learn how to see them. A photographer works to develop that knack, or vision, or alertness to possibilities, every time he or she picks up a camera. Your best teacher will be your own images. You need to take pictures—lots of them—then examine them closely and critically. Then go back and try again.

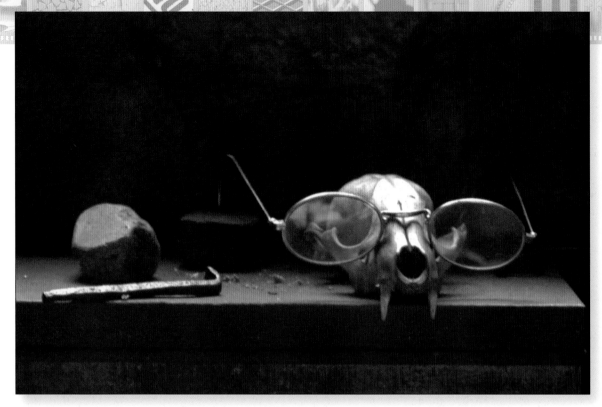

The blacksmith at an historic village rested his glasses on an old, bleached animal skull. There was just enough light inside the blacksmith's shed to make this image. The strong horizontal line of the shelf gives some structure to the random order of the objects on the shelf itself.

Some people might say this was a pretty crummy picture of the flag. We see just part of it. Only a small section of it is adequately lit, and that portion is backlit, so it is a very unusual photograph. But the red and white stripes that are lit seem to jump out from the background, and that is what I think makes this a fresh image.

There are strong lines and shapes in this image, even though the lighting is soft. There are no horizontal lines, but vertical columns of the belfry help keep viewers properly oriented in space.

An old Dodge truck would be an interesting subject anyplace. But in this condition, squeezed between two ancient stone walls, it was too good to pass up. The key to photographing mechanical things like this is usually to move in very close. You can even cut off some parts if it makes a stronger image. Look for shapes and textures. Here there are several very bold shapes—circles, rectangles, and polygons. Note how the alignment of the old shed in back of the truck seems to be part of the truck itself—a happy accident!

Oh, you say you aren't interested in haystacks or peppers or trees? It doesn't matter what you photograph, because your subject is actually the light, and how it changes the image during the day. So pick any subject that interests you—preferably one that will stay in one place all day. You say you don't want to "waste" a whole day on photography? Okay, here's an alternative. Take a pepper, or a soccer ball, or any relatively small object that you can set down on a table *indoors*. Then move a lamp (without the lampshade) around from the left to the right (better get permission first) and photograph that object with the light in half a dozen locations. Don't move the object or the camera, just the light. (You might need some assistance on this assignment.) When you are finished, compare the images. Some will be downright dull, but a couple will be pretty interesting. Then ask yourself what makes them interesting. Is it the contrast between the light and the shadow areas, or the texture that is revealed when the subject is lit strongly from one side? If the object had been a person and you were making a portrait, which would be the best place to place the light? Which would be the worst?

If some of these suggestions seem more like activities to develop your skills rather than to produce an instant masterpiece, you are catching on rapidly. The way to learn to take better photographs is to make photographs—lots of them. Then look at them critically, asking yourself some questions:

- Is the light coming from the best angle? Would the image be better if there were stronger shadows, or no shadows?

- If there is a dominant shape or a really strong color in the image, have I placed it in the best section of the picture? Would it be better if it were off to one side a bit?

- Could I get closer, or maybe focus on just a segment of the object—one small detail instead of the whole thing?

Those are the kinds of questions to ask yourself both while you are shooting and also later, when you review your images. Many times you may be able to go back and reshoot something that you know you can improve on. That's a major advantage of working in your own neighborhood. Shoot and reshoot until it seems you have exhausted the possibilities of the subject. In other words, experiment!

You're not a gardener, or even slightly interested in plants? Okay, but as a photographer, you should be interested in the shapes of the leaves and the shadows—and that, after all, is the real subject of the photo.

Five things to do with a bridge, four of them shot within a few minutes of each other from the same side of the river on a very humid morning. That's the reason for the soft light. In the fifth image, the light is harsh and in front of the camera, so the bridge structure is without any detail—just the dark forms of pylons and cables. None of the images is particularly compelling, but you can learn a lot from working over a subject from all angles and distances, and in different light. Note that in every case, there was something in the foreground.

CHAPTER 4

Orientation to Your Camera

Most of what we cover in this book is appropriate for both film and digital cameras, but in this chapter, we'll skip topics that would be of interest only to those who use film.

Digital cameras usually do things automatically that people had to do manually only a few years ago—like focus, and determine how much light was available. But other things haven't changed. There is still a lens, a viewfinder, and a shutter release (that's the little button on top that you press to take a picture). In addition, there is now an on-off switch and often a button to zoom in or zoom out. Most digital cameras also have a viewer that let's you see the image you just shot. Take a look at the labeled photos on page 58 to identify those elements. Then, if your own camera is handy, locate them there, too.

Many digital camera have built-in programs (modes) for taking portraits, landscapes, sports or action shots, and even for taking pictures at night. Although you can set your camera on *automatic*, you'll have much more control over the depth-of-field if you use the appropriate mode. Depth-of-field refers to how much of the image, from in front of your subject to in back of it, is in sharp focus. You may want to keep the background in soft focus (a little fuzzy) when you are shooting a portrait. That way, there are likely to be fewer distracting things in the background.

Controlling depth-of-field is an essential part of your craft. Any distracting elements in the background and the foreground are thrown out-of-focus when you have a short depth-of-field. You'll want to use the PORTRAIT setting on your camera (or a large aperture) when you shoot close-ups of people, flowers, or insects.

Look at the top of your camera for the dial that sets the camera for the kind of subject you're working on. One setting is probably called AUTO, and that's what most inexperienced snapshooters use. You can start out there if the camera is new to you, but soon you'll want to try the other settings.

EXPOSURE MODES		
Landscape	▲▲	mountain icon
Close-up	🌷	flower icon
Portrait	👤	head icon
Sports/Action	🏃	runner icon
Point & Shoot	📷	AUTO

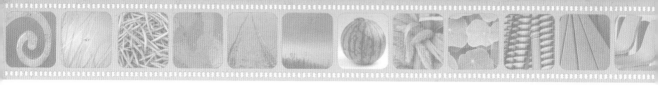

shutter release

fill flash

zoom lens

■ **Front view.** There is often a fill-flash near the top of the camera, and many cameras have a zoom lens that allows you to move in a little closer to the subject. It is usually better, however, to use your feet to move in.

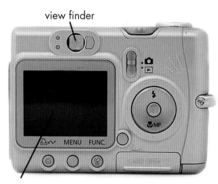

view finder

view screen

MENU   FUNC.

■ **Back view.** The major element on the back of the camera is the viewing screen. There are usually a few buttons that let you delete a poor image or view previous images, and a button to select the menu. Refer to the camera's manual to figure out how to use these features.

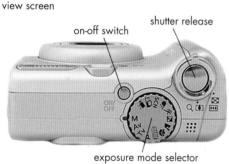

on-off switch

shutter release

exposure mode selector

■ **Top view.** Note that the shutter release is almost always in the same position on every camera. However, the on-off switch is sometimes on the front and sometimes on the back of the camera. In some cameras, there is no mode selector "wheel." In this case, the exposure setting is done from the menu.

■ The mode selector is located on the top of the camera. Here, the red arrow points to the LANDSCAPE icon. You can also find the AUTO mode (but don't use that any longer than you have to). And there is a PROGRAM mode that lets you set the aperture or the shutter speed, or both. The LANDSCAPE and PORTRAIT modes are probably the ones you'll use most often at the beginning.

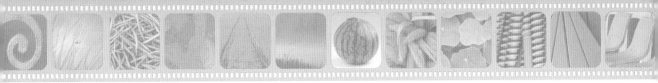

STEP BY STEP ←—————————————————————

You can take pictures even before you're comfortable with all the controls on your camera. But pretty soon you should experiment with different settings, just to see how the image you get is different when you set it first on *portrait* and then on *landscape*, for example. A lot of cameras don't permit those settings—everything is pretty automatic with some of them. But if you can, go beyond the automatic mode and fit the setting, or program, to your subject.

1 Look through the viewfinder and find a subject.

2 Move in until that subject just about fills the entire viewfinder. Notice that I suggest you move in rather than use your zoom lens. Closer is almost always better.

3 Turn the camera on its side if that helps to include everything in the viewfinder.

4 Select *portrait*, or *close-up*, or *landscape* (or other) mode, based on the nature of your subject. I suggest *landscape* unless you are really close or shooting some sports action.

5 Turn the camera on.

6 Press the shutter release slightly—about halfway. That tells the camera to measure the light on the subject and to bring it into sharpest focus.

7 Before you press the shutter release all the way, brace the camera with both hands, and take another look at your composition to be sure there is nothing distracting at the edges of the frame.

8 Now *slowly* squeeze the shutter release. Many images are blurred because the photographer punched it quickly. A *slow squeeze* is best.

9 Review the image in the viewer. Would it be better if you moved in closer? Or if you moved to the right or left a little? Is there enough light on the subject?

10 Make an adjustment and shoot another.

Sometimes the automatic features of a digital camera work against you. The autofocus may have trouble locating a subject you want in sharp focus because there's a prominent object in the foreground. The automatic light meter may give too much weight to a very bright object in the center of the viewfinder, with the result that the image overall is underexposed (too dark). When you review the image and find there's a problem, adjust a setting and shoot it again. Try to get the image right in the camera rather than attempting to fix it later on in the computer. (That's a subject for a different book.)

Some people bring their cameras to a photo store to get prints, and others upload the images to a website for display and maybe to buy prints. Most cameras come with a connection to a computer, so if you have the software, you can transfer, store, display, and print your own images. That goes beyond the scope of this book, but you can check the manual that came with your camera for information on how to store and display your images.

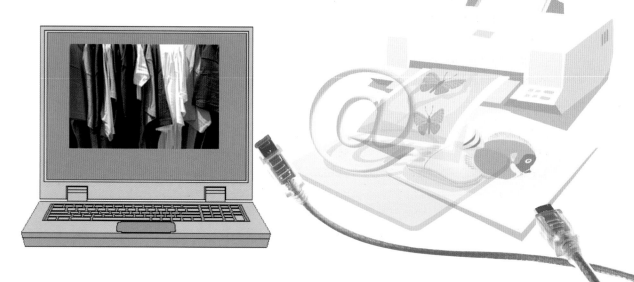

I believe that photographers should start shooting pictures as soon as possible, even before they've learned the names of all the parts of the camera. So we've skipped a lot of terms like *aperture* and *f-stop* so that you can get out there and make pictures. A few terms that all experienced photographers use are included in the glossary, so if it's raining or snowing out right now, you can check out those words. At this stage, memorizing them will not improve your photography, and there's no vocabulary test for this book!

A FEW ADDITIONAL TIPS AND A CLOSING POINT

- Digital cameras require batteries, and batteries can be drained quickly if you do a lot of zooming in and out, or if you spend gobs of time reviewing your images and showing them to others. They drain even faster if you leave the camera turned on when you are just walking around looking for something to shoot.

- Always check to see that your lens cap is off when you get ready to shoot and that no dust has gotten on the lens. If there is dust, blow it off or wipe gently with a soft brush or cloth—*never* use your finger to brush it off. You may scratch the lens, and you have oil on your skin that smears the image.

- Camera straps and long hair have a nasty habit of hanging down in front of the lens, so always hold on to them, or check to make sure they are not in front of the camera when you compose your image.

Technical and creative control are both essential for great images, and neither comes quickly. There is much more you will need to master before you can consistently take fine images. Your camera's manual has more information about exposure, f-stops and shutter settings, and other shooting modes. Time spent reading it carefully is never wasted.

We talked in this book about the creative aspects of the craft of photography, but that does not mean the technical aspects can be neglected. You will be better able to deal with the technical controls when you see in your own images why an understanding of *depth-of-field* and *exposure* are important. Actually, technical control is essential to achieve what you had in mind when you pointed your camera at a certain subject in the first place. But there's no reason to sit around the house waiting for that level of technical control to arrive. So get out there now and make some pictures!

Glossary of Photographic Terms

aperture is the variable opening in the lens that lets light into the camera. It is expressed as an f-stop number. The lower the f-stop number, the larger the aperture.

aperture priority mode lets the photographer set the aperture, and then the camera automatically selects the shutter speed. Use this when you want to control the depth-of-field.

ASA (or ISO) is a system for rating the sensitivity to light of film or the photocells in a digital camera. Most digital cameras today use the ISO rating designation, which is identical. An ISO (or ASA) rating of 100 means the film or camera's sensitivity is lower than one set at an ASA/ISO of 800. But a low ASA/ISO usually results in a smoother appearance with less "grain." See also *ISO*.

backlight is the light that project towards the camera from behind the principal subject.

bracketing means making additional exposures that are both 1 or 2 f-stops over and 1 or 2 f-stops under the indicated exposure. Use this when the lighting is difficult to judge.

contrast in photography is the difference between the brilliant (or light) and the dense (dark) areas of an image. A high-contrast image is one with both very bright white/highlights and very deep shadows. A low-contrast image (such as you might get on a foggy morning) would have no highlights and perhaps no entirely black areas.

convergence means that two (or more) lines or edges appear to come together in the distance, even though in reality they are parallel when viewed up close. The best examples are a railroad track and a skyscraper.

depth-of-field is an area extending both in front of and behind the point of sharpest focus in which the subject is acceptably sharp. For a landscape, you generally want a large (or deep) depth of field (everything in focus). For

a portrait, you may prefer a short depth-of-field (all but the subject's face slightly out of focus). To maximize the depth of field, set the camera at its smallest aperture (f/22 or greater) and focus about one-third of the way up from the bottom of your picture.

exposure is the total light reaching the film. It is determined by several things: the luminance (brightness) of the subject, the aperture setting, the shutter speed, and the film speed (the ASA/ISO rating). Photographers often say, "increase the exposure by one f-stop," or "stop down by two f-stops." You can increase the exposure by using a larger aperture or by using a slower shutter speed.

film speed is a measure of a film's sensitivity to light. Faster films tend to have more grain and less resolving power (sharpness in the edges).

f-stop is a measure of the aperture opening. An f-stop of 8 admits twice the amount of light as an f-stop of 11. The f-stop numbering system is initially confusing because the smaller the number, the larger the aperture. F-stops are sequenced in this manner: 1.4, 2, 2.8, 4, 5.6, 8, 11, 16, 22, etc. Increasing the f-stop by one stop (say from f /8 to f/11) halves the light reaching the film; decreasing the aperture by one f-stop (say from f/16 to f/11) doubles the amount of light.

fill-flash is a controlled amount of flash used to brighten deep shadow areas, usually when working in bright sunlight. It lightens up areas in shadow and reduces the contrast. Most cameras include a fill-flash mode that forces the flash to fire, even in bright light.

horizon is the generally level line where the earth and sky seem to meet. In the plains of Kansas, a viewer might see it as a perfectly flat line, but in the mountains of Colorado, one might have to infer the horizon.

ISO is a system for rating the sensitivity to light of film. It has been adopted by digital camera makers to indicate the relative sensitivity of the camera setting. Most digital cameras today use the ISO designation instead of the ASA designation, but the meaning of two terms is identical for our purposes. An ISO (or ASA) rating of 100 means the film or camera's sensitivity setting is less than one set at 800. Not all cameras permit adjustment of the ISO. If they do, one is well-advised to keep the setting rather low, as the color saturation and contrast are reduced with high settings.

opaque is a characteristic that makes something resist the passage of light. See also translucent.

overexposure means there was too much light striking the photosensitive material. Underexposure means there was too little light for a good image.

perspective is the representation of a three-dimensional object (like a flower vase sitting on a table) in two-dimensions, such as in a photograph or painting.

shutter is a mechanical system in a camera for controlling the amount of time of the exposure.

shutter priority mode is a setting available on more expensive cameras that lets the photographer set the shutter, and the camera automatically selects the aperture. Use this when you want to "stop" the action, or when you want to show the motion blur of a sports scene or a waterfall, for example.

shutter release is the button that you press to take the picture.

shutter speed is the amount of time the shutter is open during the exposure. A typical combination for many landscape photographers might be a shutter speed of 1/60 of a second and an f-stop of f/16, assuming one has a reasonably bright day and an ISO of 100–200. The standard sequence for both digital and film cameras is 1, 2, 4, 8, 15, 30, 60, 125, 250, 1000..., where 60 represents 1/60 of a second, 125 represents 1/125 second, and so on.

soft focus is a blurred or slightly out-of-focus image, often done deliberately to create a special mood.

translucent is a characteristic of a material (such as a screen or fabric) that is neither clear nor transparent, but that will allow a certain amount of light to pass through it. If no light can pass through, the material is opaque.

viewfinder is a device on a camera for sighting and framing the image to be photographed.